TRANSFORMED

IRON HILL

press

TRANSFORMED

Embracing the Death of Self and the Power of God

Rick Burgess

IRON HILL
press

Transformed: Embracing the Death of Self and the Power of God

Published by Iron Hill Press in the United States of America.

ISBN 13: 9798985749816

"Now may the God of peace himself sanctify you completely, and may your whole spirit and soul and body be kept blameless at the coming of our Lord Jesus Christ."

1 THESSALONIANS 5:23

CONTENTS

INTRODUCTION

The fastest growing "religion" in our country right now is the worship of self. But, of course, this has been an issue with human beings from the beginning. How did Satan convince Adam and Eve to eat from the tree of the knowledge of good and evil? By convincing Eve that God couldn't be trusted to decide right from wrong. The Tempter said that Adam and Eve should be able to determine that for themselves. "Did God really say you will die if you disobey Him? Surely not." And so they rebelled against God, and from that moment until now, sin separates God and His creation.

But that's also when we see the first inkling of God's plan to redeem humankind from their sins. We chose to elevate ourselves to be our own gods, but Jesus took on human flesh and came to us when we could not come to Him. The Son of God came to redeem all who believe in Him, repent of their sins, and submit to His authority. If we are sincere in this belief, God makes us fully righteous. We are justified. We are sanctified.

Unfortunately, many see this as the end. But Jesus said it was a new beginning. Jesus was and is counter-cultural. In Luke 9:23 and Mathew 16:24, Jesus told all who desired to be His disciples that they must deny themselves and pick up a cross. To truly live, we must die to ourselves! Too often, we read the words and foolishly think this means becoming a "better" version of ourselves. That is not what Jesus is saying. He is saying our old self is dead, and now we have become transformed into a new self in Christ. Jesus says in John 15:5 we must abide in His power in order to bear much fruit because apart from Him, we can do nothing! He goes on in 15:8 to say that this fruit He produces in us proves that we are His disciples.

To follow Jesus faithfully, we must be rooted in Him. This is the image of the tree on the cover of this book. The tree is dead at the top, just as we must embrace the death of our "selves." But the closer we get to the roots, the closer we get to the source of our strength; we are renewed with Spirit-fueled, Christ-centered life. When we abide in Christ, we seek Him, pursuing righteousness, godliness, faith, and endurance as Paul instructed Timothy (1 Timothy 6:11). As we grow in our sanctification and remain attached to the source, we mature and grow spiritually. When we are completely rooted in Christ, we produce much new fruit and prove we are His disciples. We die to ourselves and are transformed by Christ. It is a powerful picture.

I was reading "The Spirit of the Disciplines" by Dallas Willard, and something he wrote jumped off the page. Willard feared that we, the Western Church, have been selling short the power of the Gospel. Willard's concern resonated with me. G.K. Chesterton echoed a similar theme when he wrote, "Christianity has not so much been tried and found wanting, as it has been found difficult and left untried." Many Christians today seem to be plagued with a lack-luster faith, one that lacks power and action.

It is true that we can do nothing to save ourselves from the consequences of our sins. We are saved from our sins by God's grace through faith alone. The Apostle Paul makes it clear that we have done nothing to warrant God's grace: "But God shows his love for us in that while we were still sinners, Christ died for us" (Romans 5:8). It is a biblical fact that we can do nothing to redeem ourselves. But the Bible paints a picture of saving faith as active faith.

Saving faith is a faith of action. What do I mean by this? First, Scripture teaches that we must repent of our sins. This isn't an additional command, something added to saving faith. It is wrapped up in saving faith. In Acts chapter 2, we find Peter, now full of the Holy Spirit, preaching a message at Pentecost that God used to cut the hearts of all who heard it. Acts 2:37-38 tells us that upon hearing the truth of the Gospel message, the people responded to Peter, "Brothers, what shall we do?"

Peter did not say, "You know? That's a great question. I don't know."

He didn't say, "Go home and let God work it out."

Peter never hesitated. "Repent and be baptized every one of you in the name of Jesus Christ for the forgiveness of your sins, and you will receive the gift of the Holy Spirit."

Their response showed Peter that they believed the truth of the Gospel message. When asked what to do next, Peter told them: Repent! Take action! Turn away from your sins and turn toward Jesus Christ for redemption. Watch your dead spirit be made alive by God's Holy Spirit!

You see, apart from Christ, we are dead in our sins. But when we come to saving faith in Jesus, we are reborn. We are made new. In a word, we are transformed.

We are transformed by faith, not by works. But as James says, the active nature of our faith is proof of our transformation. We look to the Old Testament long before Jesus burst onto the scene and see men like Noah and Abraham. These men had a faith that led God to declare them righteous. But how was their faith measured? Abraham wasn't deemed righteous solely because he believed God told him to go. His faith was proven legitimate because he went. Abraham had a faith of action! Noah wasn't deemed righteous only because he believed God wanted him to build the ark. He was deemed righteous because he methodically built the ark by following God's instructions to the letter. Noah had a faith of action!

We are transformed by our faith in Christ alone through the work of Christ on the cross. But this transformation involves repentance from our sins, surrendering faith in our ability to justify ourselves, and placing our hope for redemption solely in Jesus. When we do so, He becomes Our Lord, our authority, and God's Holy Spirit replaces our dead spirit. This transformation continues until our earthly death or the return of Jesus Christ, when we will all be glorified.

When we are saved by faith, we are justified in Jesus Christ and made fully righteous. In what is a profound and wonderful mystery, we are sanctified, i.e., made holy, in God's eyes, and also begin the process of sanctification, i.e., growing in our Christ-likeness. All under the power and leading of the Holy Spirit. This devotion you hold in your hands will concentrate on the sanctification process described in Scripture. The Bible teaches us that those that are truly redeemed are being completely transformed into something that they were not before. We'll unpack this process over the next month and examine what it means for our lives.

Before we move on, I need to ask you: Have you been transformed? Do you see the drastic change in your life that only God can bring about? If we claim to be "saved," but we have not been and are not being transformed, then we are saying that somehow the power that raised Jesus from the dead has now entered our life, but it did not have much impact on us at all. Brothers, if God hasn't transformed you and isn't actively transforming you, it is not because He cannot do so.

If you arrive at this point in this introduction and do not recognize yourself in the description of what it means to be saved by faith, the best thing you can do now is to examine your relationship with God and ask Him, in prayer, where you stand with Him. The transformation brought about through saving faith is life-bringing. Without the salvation only God can offer, you stand separated from the nearly limitless blessings of God. Before moving on in this book, I would ask you to evaluate your life and do any work you need to do to get right with God. Too much is at stake for this to be left in the balance.

For those of you reading this who are confident that God's grace has saved you through faith, are you willing to take the next 31 days to allow God's Word to pose some challenging questions? If so, let's find out if our lives truly reflect the transformation available only in the redeeming power of the Almighty God.

Has God transformed you? Is He transforming you? It's an honor to join you as we answer these questions together.

DAY 1
WHAT DO YOU VALUE?

"[7] But whatever gain I had, I counted as loss for the sake of Christ. [8] Indeed, I count everything as loss because of the surpassing worth of knowing Christ Jesus my Lord. For his sake I have suffered the loss of all things and count them as rubbish, in order that I may gain Christ."
- PHILIPPIANS 3:7–8

When I was a "cultural Christian," I had to pretend to be interested in the things of God when in reality, the things of the world were much more interesting to me. When Christ redeemed me, I began to notice that things I once deemed valuable had lost their luster. But this transformation took time.

When I finally surrendered my life to Christ, I wondered how it would affect my work. I do a secular radio show, and on the show, we talk about a variety of things, including much about our personal life. My first pastor encouraged me to work my faith into the show's content. Early in my walk with Christ, it was difficult because I was still much more interested in the world than in my faith. I knew so little about the God who had redeemed me.

Sure, I knew the basic stuff I had been taught while growing up in the Bible Belt. But I had no real understanding or love for God's Word. I pretended to be interested in sharing my faith on the show. But I was most excited about the next funny thing I could say on the show because that was my true passion and desire. At this point in my life, I struggled when the Holy Spirit prompted me to speak about my Lord and Savior.

Then a transformation began to take place. The more I worshipped, prayed, and learned the Bible, the more wonderful it all became. Twenty-six years later, I can honestly say with zero hesitation that Christ has so transformed me that instead of pretending to be interested in the things of God, I have to force myself to pretend to care about anything else. I just don't find things in this world that interesting or desirable compared to what I have in Christ.

The Apostle Paul talks about this in Philippians 3:7–8. Before Christ transformed Paul, people loved him. He was highly educated, wealthy, had the best seats in the Temple, and was revered both for his zeal for God and his persecution of the disciples of Jesus. But then Paul had an encounter with Jesus and was radically transformed. God made Paul a new man. God would use the same Paul who had persecuted the Church to grow the Church.

This transformation cost Paul, and it will cost us. Paul said that due to his devotion to Christ, he lost the things of the world he once had. But since he truly met Jesus, he considered anything he may have lost to be garbage compared to what he had gained.

Transformation changes your standard for what is truly valuable and what isn't. I remember thinking football games and deer hunting were far more valuable to me than a Bible study, mission trip, or making disciples. Today I can honestly say that while I still enjoy those things, I do not worship those things. Why? Because compared to the surpassing worth of knowing Jesus Christ and advancing His Kingdom, these things have lost their luster. Nothing is better than knowing Jesus.

FOR REFLECTION

Are there things in your life you still value more than knowing Christ? If so, these things are inhibiting your transformation. Do what it takes to rightly order the things you value most in life.

DAY 2
THE SECRET TO LIFE

"[21] For to me to live is Christ, and to die is gain. [22] If I am to live in the flesh, that means fruitful labor for me. Yet which I shall choose I cannot tell. [23] I am hard pressed between the two. My desire is to depart and be with Christ, for that is far better." -PHILIPPIANS 1:21-23

What is the secret to life? You can exhaust yourself searching for the world's attempts to answer this question. Every solution the world offers falls flat because they are rooted in our fallen creation. But Paul figured this out a long time ago. How? Because Jesus had transformed him, he understood that the secret to life is to live in service to Christ.

Paul wasn't serving Christ to earn his redemption; he was serving Christ because of his redemption. His priorities had been transformed to the point that he realized that knowing Jesus is so wonderful that you can get to the point where you really can't lose. If you live, you get to stay on earth to serve Christ to follow His commands. You get to be about the business of being and making disciples as instructed by the Lord. Far from being a burden, this service is a joy. Unlike the useless work of the world that never quite satisfies, this work has eternal consequences and reward.

We see in Philippians 1:21-23 that Paul had come to the place where he realized that if he were allowed to live, he would live to serve Christ. And if he lost his earthly life while serving Jesus, he then would be in the presence of Christ, which is even better! Paul appreciated the gift of life on earth but realized when it ends, then eternal life with Christ is even better. Paul wasn't going to end his life on his timeline because he'd been transformed; he viewed his life differently than before he encountered Jesus.

Paul knew his life didn't belong to him since he had been transformed through faith in Christ. God had bought him through Jesus' sacrifice on the cross. Therefore, Paul realized that if his Lord thought it was better for him to stay and advance the Kingdom, he would submit to that call. But Paul also knew that if God decided to end his earthly life and ministry, the results of that sovereign decision would even be better.

Paul was hard pressed between two desires: fulfilling God's plan for him on this earth or joining God eternally in Heaven. But Paul was committed to whatever God deemed best because Paul no longer considered his agenda to be more important than God's agenda. He had found the secret to life: to live is to serve Christ, and to die is to be in the presence of Christ! The transformed win either way.

Is your life devoted to advancing the Kingdom of God? God has transformed me to the point where I can say, without hesitation, that if my work does not point people to Jesus, it has been a monumental waste of time. Sadly, this has not always been my conviction. But because Jesus Christ transformed me, I no longer see value in seeing my life's work glorifying me. The only value to my life is whether it is used to glorify Him.

FOR REFLECTION

Christ has transformed you. How has this changed how you answer the question, "What is the secret to life"? Paul reminds us elsewhere in Scripture that whatever we do, we must do it with all our hearts as if we're doing it for the Lord and not for others. Why? Because we can know that if we do so, we will receive an inheritance as our reward (Colossians 3:23–24). How does Christ transform our life's work? By reminding us that the redeemed serve Him. How does this help you to see your life and work differently?

DAY 3

TOTAL SUBMISSION

"Put to death therefore what is earthly in you: sexual immorality, impurity, passion, evil desire, and covetousness, which is idolatry." -COLOSSIANS 3:5

The pastor God used to help save my life spoke to me the way Paul spoke to the Church at Colossae in Colossians 3:5. I had claimed to be a Christian from when I was a little boy. I was a pretty good kid compared to the other children around me. The same held for much of my teenage years. I attended church, but I was not immersed in church. (Attending church isn't the same as being involved in church.) I wasn't an agnostic or an atheist; I believed in God. I believed He sent His son, Jesus, to die on the cross to forgive me of my sins. I believed that if I wasn't "saved," I would go to hell. So, when I was around 10, I responded to an altar call, asked God to forgive me of my sins, and was baptized soon after.

But late in high school, I struggled with sins I couldn't control. So, like many of the people my age at the time, I responded to another altar call and got baptized again. Why? Because I wasn't living a transformed life. Unfortunately, by age 19, I had stopped attending church. I spent the 12 years after that living a life of deliberate and perpetual sin.

When I met my wife, Sherri, and we desired to be married, we went to find a church where we could have the ceremony. We chose a church, and when we met with the pastor, he asked me why I wanted to get married in his church. I replied that the church was the most convenient location for our families. Imagine my surprise when he told me that he would not marry Sherri and me because I was lost. This did not sit well with me, and I asked him what gave him the right to declare me lost. He boldly replied that it wasn't he who declared me lost; the lack of transformation in my life told him I was lost. He correctly pointed out that I was living a life of sin. I wasn't merely making mistakes, coming under conviction, and repenting. No, I lived a lifestyle of sin.

The disciple of Christ will always struggle with his sinful nature. But a disciple of Jesus, as Paul states in today's Scripture, doesn't live a life of deliberate sin. Paul says that the redeemed once walked in a lifestyle of sin, but they don't anymore. Paul says the wrath of God is coming on those who do not repent and continue to live a life of sin. He says we must put sin to death because we are being transformed through the power of the Spirit. He says to put sin away. This is the action-oriented faith of the Bible.

This call to a new life isn't the call to become a somewhat better version of our old self. Jesus says in Luke 9:23 that His disciples must deny themselves and pick up their cross daily. This means the old you is dead. You are not a better version of your old self but a new self that is now selfless in Christ.

This is what the pastor was pointing out to me so many years ago. He did not see a transformed man sitting in front of him. And I knew he was right. I left that meeting, went home, and got out my Bible. God led me to James 4:7–8, a passage that changed my life: "[7] Submit yourselves therefore to God. Resist the devil, and he will flee from you. [8] Draw near to God, and he will draw near to you. Cleanse your hands, you sinners, and purify your hearts, you double-minded." I will never forget that moment.

I couldn't understand why I had not been transformed until that moment. Sitting on my floor, Bible open in front of me, I was convinced by the truth that I was still living as if I was under my authority. Though I believed in Jesus, I did not belong to Jesus. I did not love Jesus; my faith was still in me, not Him. Realizing this, I submitted to His authority, repented from my sins, turned from the devil, and put my faith in God. At that moment, God came near to me and began the process of completely transforming my life.

FOR REFLECTION

Has Jesus truly transformed your life? Do you still see sin that should not be there in your life? Do you live a lifestyle of sin? Maybe you need to submit to God today, resist the devil and sin in your life, and come near to God. Trust that He is faithful and will draw near to you.

DAY 4
ONCE, BUT NO LONGER

"And such were some of you. But you were washed, you were sanctified, you were justified in the name of the Lord Jesus Christ and by the Spirit of our God."

-1 CORINTHIANS 6:11

The Apostle Paul was getting reports from the Church at Corinth that he did not like. He planted this church in one of the world's most sinful cities. Many theologians believe that Paul wrote his letter to the Romans during his time in Corinth. Paul was looking at this sinful city and wondering why the sin outside the church was now creeping its way into the church.

John Phillips says the Church is like a boat on the water. The boat is fine when it's floating on the water. The problem arises when the water outside the boat begins to come inside and causes it to sink. The Church can exist in the world, but the problem arises when the Church begins to become of the world. Even inside the Church, too many times, sin isn't taken seriously.

How often have you heard someone say, "God meets us right where we are"? While it is true that God is willing to redeem us right where we are, He certainly doesn't leave us there. He delivers us from open, deliberate, and perpetual sin.

Take a moment and read 1 Corinthians 6:9-11. Look what Paul is saying to the sinners in the church. Verse 11 is key here: "And such were some of you." Paul rolls out a list of sins that, if left unredeemed, will deny entrance into the Kingdom of God. But then Paul reminds and reassures those in his audience who have been redeemed by saving faith in Christ that this is how they were before they were redeemed.

Have you ever noticed when Christians look at a list of sins like the one we see in verses 9-10 that we are often very vocal about the sins on the list that we don't struggle with? It's as if we have decided that some of these sins are important while others are not as important. Paul is helping us see that none of the sins on this list are any greater than the others. None of them require some sort of extra level of redemption on God's part. But it's also true that none of them get a pass. Every sin on this list requires outside intervention in order to redeem us. And that intervention is accomplished in the person and work of Jesus Christ. Every one of us who is currently saved by faith in Jesus once was dead in our sin. But through faith in Christ, we were washed, we were justified, and we were sanctified by the Lord Jesus and the very Spirit of God Himself. Paul was reminding the Corinthians that this was the life they once lived, so why in the world would they live it again? The same question applies to us.

Do you see yourself creeping back to sins of the past? Why? While we will always struggle with sin, returning to sinful habits God delivered us from is an insult to God. Paul is reminding us that for those who have been transformed, there is no room for any of the baggage of habitual sin to creep back into our lives. Remember, while we were once that way, thanks to the power of the gracious God we serve, we are no longer that way. We have been transformed, and we are being transformed.

FOR REFLECTION

If you find yourself drifting back into old sin habits, ask yourself why. Have you abandoned your time in Scripture? Has your prayer life taken a hit? Are you drifting back into a place that God has clearly delivered you from? Are there people in your life who should not be in your inner circle? Spend time evaluating your spiritual habits today.

DAY 5
NO LONGER A SLAVE

"'All things are lawful for me,' but not all things are helpful. 'All things are lawful for me,' but I will not be dominated by anything." -1 CORINTHIANS 6:12

Many Christ-followers have a tendency to show the world how free they can be in Christ. In 1 Corinthians 6:12, Paul instructs us to be careful when testing these boundaries. Just because we are saved by grace through faith doesn't mean that we can do whatever we want and trust God's grace to cover it. There are many places in Scripture, many of them covered in this book, where the scriptures show us that once we are redeemed, we are bent toward pursuing Spirit-fueled holiness. The transformation that occurs when we come to faith in Christ leads us to want to obey Jesus' commands. A disciple says what Christ says to say and does what Christ says to do. Jesus said clearly in John 14 that those who love Him actually strive to obey Him. So Paul isn't saying that we are no longer called to follow the commands of God.

What Paul means in this verse is that there are areas of life where what we are about to do isn't sin, but it is still unwise. Although we may be free in Christ to do it, it doesn't mean that we can't still abuse the freedom to the point that our actions become sinful. The example he uses in the very next verse is food. In 1 Corinthians 6:13, Paul says, "'Food is meant for the stomach and the stomach for food'—and God will destroy both one and the other." What is Paul talking about here?

Scripture teaches that we eat to live but must not live to eat. This doesn't mean that we can't enjoy food, but we do know that we can overindulge in food to the point of gluttony. This was a big problem for me when I was first redeemed and committed to following Jesus. I would abuse the freedom given to me in Christ to eat whatever foods I enjoyed. I had to learn that I was not free to set a bad example or damage my witness by overeating to the point that I lost all self-control. It's one thing to enjoy food, but it's another to be addicted to food and treat our bodies with disregard. I can tell you that I never addressed my relationship with food until the Holy Spirit convicted me that it was a sin. I began to lose weight by exercising and eating less when I was finally willing to admit that I had abused my freedom to the point of sin.

The consumption of alcohol is another place that Christ-followers stumble. There are different views on alcohol consumption within the Church, and this isn't the proper platform to flesh those differing views out. But I believe all Christians can say with no reservation that the Bible is unequivocal in its view that drunkenness is a sin. And one way that many Christians safeguard against abusing their freedom in Christ is to resist being a "sin daredevil" with alcohol.

Paul's sums up how we should view our liberty in Christ. Out of love for our fellow Brothers and Sisters, we should sacrifice our freedom in order to never do anything in front of others that makes them uncomfortable, offends them, or tempts them to sin. That means that you may lovingly limit your freedom to consume alcohol in front of people who may have a conviction toward drinking. Or that you refrain from eating certain foods in front of people who may be offended by the consumption of a certain food.

The heart of this passage is where Paul says, "but I will not be dominated by anything." Some translations use the word "enslaved." What a powerful truth. There should be nothing that owns us to the point that we cannot give it up for the glory of God. Is there anything you would not sacrifice for a stronger witness for Christ?

Sometimes we make the mistake of thinking that our transformation means that God will give us our desires when in reality, transformation brings a changing of our desires. As we are being transformed, we grow closer to a point where the things of this world just lose their luster. God and the things of God are so superior to the things of this world that we grow to a place where they just don't measure up. Along the way, we often learn that our freedom in Christ is best used to glorify Him in a state of discernment and discipline consistent with our identities as new creations in Christ.

FOR REFLECTION

We must be very careful with our freedom. Some things and hobbies were too important to me at one time, and God put those things in their proper place. I will not be enslaved by anything. Where do you stand? While you are free to enjoy responsibly, are there practices and behaviors that distract from your pursuit of God and your efforts to lead others to Him?

DAY 6

HEAVEN FOCUSED

"[20] But our citizenship is in heaven, and from it we await a Savior, the Lord Jesus Christ, [21] who will transform our lowly body to be like his glorious body, by the power that enables him even to subject all things to himself."
-PHILIPPIANS 3:20-21

One of the classic mistakes Christians make is trying to create Heaven here on earth. The reason people do this is that they haven't grown up spiritually.

How would you describe your life? Do you live a Heaven-focused life? Or are you clinging to this world to the point that if you were honest, you consider Heaven to be a let-down to you unless certain things of this world will be present there? If this describes you, this is a dangerous place to be because it can lead to major disappointment and disillusionment. Creation needs redemption, just as we do. Our world is fallen; perfection will never be found on this side of Heaven. If your joy is based on circumstances, you have just stepped on a roller coaster of never-ending ups and downs.

When we are in the process of being transformed, the Holy Spirit begins to create in us a heaven-focused life. My wife, Sherri, and I experienced this shift when our youngest son died his earthly death at the precious age of two and a half years old. This highlighted the problem with a life that is trying to create Heaven in a fallen creation. If our goal was "Heaven on earth," then the day our son died his earthly death, our pursuit of Heaven on earth would have been over.

Be careful with equating things you may enjoy on earth with what you imagine Heaven will be like. Notice what Paul is saying in Philippians 3:20-21. He said we wait for our Lord, our Savior, to transform our bodies into a body like His, who is in need of nothing. Our reward in Heaven isn't more of our favorite foods, the hobbies we enjoyed, the sports teams we foolishly worshipped, or even the earthly family and friends we loved. No, to live a Heaven-focused life is to have the desire to be in the presence of God the Father and to live as co-heirs alongside Jesus. Can you imagine? Unlike this fallen creation that is fading away, God promises a new creation in eternity with Him. He has conquered death; one day, He will remove our mourning, crying, and pain (Revelation 21). All the former things that bring us so much shame will be removed, and all things will be made perfect!

When God finally calls all His children to Himself for eternity, everything will be made right. For the first time in our lives, you and I will experience things as they were always meant to be before the fall of creation. Do you realize what that means? The most beautiful thing you have ever seen on this fallen earth is a throwaway due to sin. Every experience you could imagine on this fallen earth will seem like nothing compared to perfection. This world is tainted and groaning to be redeemed. But God has promised that for Believers, everything will be made right.

I'll close this devotional by paraphrasing something C.S. Lewis wrote in his powerful book, "Mere Christianity." Lewis pointed out that to the unredeemed, the fallen earth will be the only Heaven they will ever see. But for Believers, this fallen earth will be the only hell we will ever see. We have been bought by the sacrifice of Jesus Christ and are now citizens of Heaven. We are no longer citizens of this fallen creation. Remember this, and it will serve you well.

FOR REFLECTION

Do you have a Heaven-focused life? Do the things of the world still intrigue you more than the things of Heaven? Hold on to the promise of Heaven by remembering the days when this fallen creation has produced yet another disappointment. Just think: this isn't such a big deal compared to eternity. Stop trying to live out Heaven on earth; live in a way on earth that prepares you to live in Heaven with Jesus.

DAY 7
TWO ROADS

"[13] Enter by the narrow gate. For the gate is wide and the way is easy that leads to destruction, and those who enter by it are many. [14] For the gate is narrow and the way is hard that leads to life, and those who find it are few."
-MATTHEW 7:13-14

The Marines have a slogan, "The few. The proud. The Marines." But this concept of "the few" was around long before the United States Marine Corps. In Matthew 7:13-14, Jesus is nearing the end of His Sermon on the Mount, informing anyone who has chosen to follow Jesus in saving faith what they should expect. Jesus paints the picture of two roads. Jesus uses three words to describe this first road. Let's focus on those words for a moment.

The words Jesus used in verse 13 are "wide, easy, and many." Jesus said that there is a wide and easy road, and most people will choose this road. What did Jesus mean by "wide"? The wide road allows room for almost anything you want to do. It is easy to navigate. There are no well-defined lines to maneuver around or through. It's just a wide road; traveling on it doesn't require much experience or focus.

What did Jesus mean by "easy"? The road is easy because it requires no real sacrifice. There is no need for discipline or self-control on this road. It's so wide that traveling on it is quite easy.

What did Jesus mean when He said that many people would take this road? Simple. It's a journey with no potholes, obstacles, or real requirements. In the moment, it seems easy. It requires little. And most people will choose that which requires the least from them. Why wouldn't everyone want this road? It's no wonder. It's preferred by most. It's so wide and easy. It doesn't feature any opposition.

Of course, Jesus used this road as a metaphor for living apart from a saving relationship with Him. He was using it as an illustration of the untransformed life. But Jesus loves us so much that He is willing to warn us that this road will lead to a destination called destruction. Jesus calls those willing to turn from that road and its perceived ease and follow Him. Jesus describes this road in verse 14.

Jesus says that those who follow Him must enter a narrow gate that leads to a difficult way. In verse 14, Jesus used three words to describe this road. He said it's narrow and hard, and only a few are willing to go this way. To many, the choice seems simple. Choose the road that is easy, wide, and populated by the masses or the one that is narrow, difficult, and traveled only by the few. Fortunately, Jesus informs us of the difference in the destinations of these two roads. Jesus says that taking the difficult, narrow road will lead to a transformed life like nothing we could experience anywhere else.

Which road are you on? Does your life look like most people or like only a few people? Do you follow the Spirit, which can be difficult, or do you feed the flesh, which feels quite easy? Are you living for the day or living for eternity?

When it comes to our salvation, the Marines have it wrong. Jesus said it correctly when He said, "the few, the humble, my disciples." Most won't choose the road to transformation because it requires dying to self and devotion to Jesus Christ. He is the only hope to correctly navigate the road that leads to life. To the willing few, they reach the proper destination, which is eternal life with Christ.

FOR REFLECTION

How would you describe the road you're on? If you have been saved by faith in Jesus Christ, you have been set on the narrow road to salvation. But maybe you're living your life as if you're on the wide road. Be careful how you move forward. What does how you live your life say about the nature of the road you are on?

DAY 8

SELF-DENIAL

"[23] And he said to all, 'If anyone would come after me, let him deny him-
self and take up his cross daily and follow me. [24] For whoever would save
his life will lose it, but whoever loses his life for my sake will save it. [25]
For what does it profit a man if he gains the whole world and loses or forfeits
himself'"? -LUKE 9:23-25

The word Christian only appears in Scripture three times in the New Testament: Acts 11:26, Acts 26:28, and 1 Peter 4:16. This was a derogatory word used to make fun of those who claimed to have found the Messiah. People mocked them for claiming to be Christ-like or "little Messiahs." Peter finally instructs the Church to use this term as a badge of honor, not as something they should be ashamed of. Peter says in 1 Peter 4:16 that if you suffer for being called a Christian, then glorify God.

Author Dallas Willard cautions us about labeling just anyone a Christian. Willard correctly points out that the word "disciple" is used 250 times in the New Testament and that everyone who was called a Christian in the New Testament Church was already a disciple. Jesus had transformed them, and their lives testified to this truth. They were worthy of being called Christians.

The Western Church seems too willing to call people Christians who have shown no evidence of being a disciple. Jesus doesn't call us Christians; He calls us disciples. He doesn't command us to make Christians; He commands us to make disciples and teach them all He has commanded.

Jesus tells us what being a disciple will require from us in Luke 9:23-25. He said that to be disciples, we must follow Him by denying ourselves and taking up our cross daily. What did Jesus mean when He said this? Let's first talk about what He did not mean. Jesus didn't imply that becoming disciples would make us a better version of ourselves. Denying ourselves means that we no longer exist. This is the transformation the Scriptures speak of, brothers! Jesus doesn't sort of change us or make us somewhat different. No, there is no longer a "you" or an "I." When we come to saving faith in Jesus, our lives are hidden in Christ (as Paul says in Colossians 3:3). Instead of the world seeing "Rick," my identity is transformed to "Rick, in Christ." I no longer exist; being hidden in Christ changes everything.

Next, Jesus tells us that even though He has made my dead spirit alive during the process of sanctification, my flesh is still alive. Therefore, I must daily pick up my cross. What does this mean? Jesus uses a visual that the disciples often saw during the reign of the Roman Empire. When they saw someone carrying a cross, they knew that person would die. The cross analogy does not represent our unique burdens or struggles. It represents our daily death to self.

Notice what Jesus says next. He tells us that if we are willing to give up our former lives, He can save us. If we desire to hold on to our old, sinful selves, then we are not truly repentant and will lose our life. Every one of us has a choice. We can choose to live for the world and lose our souls or follow Jesus in faith and repentance, gaining abundant life on this earth and eternal life forever with God. It's that simple.

FOR REFLECTION

Have you made this choice? Do you see the evidence of Christ flowing from your life? Do you truly believe that a life in Christ is better than a life in the world? How does your life bear witness to your identity as a disciple?

DAY 9
RECOGNIZED

"[13] Now when they saw the boldness of Peter and John, and perceived that they were uneducated, common men, they were astonished. And they recognized that they had been with Jesus . . . [18] So they called them and charged them not to speak or teach at all in the name of Jesus. [19] But Peter and John answered them, 'Whether it is right in the sight of God to listen to you rather than to God, you must judge, [20] for we cannot but speak of what we have seen and heard.'" -ACTS 4:13, 18-20

What a change we notice in the lives of Peter and John! Aren't these two the same men who abandoned Jesus in the garden when the Jewish leaders and the Roman soldiers showed up to arrest Him? Once Peter found out that Jesus wasn't going to defend Himself, he abandoned Jesus and was so afraid of being associated with Him that he began to lie about knowing Jesus, to the point that he was swearing and cussing at being called one of His followers. But in Acts 4, Luke tells us that the Jewish leaders saw Peter and John's boldness and connected it with the fact that they had been in the company of Jesus. What changed? Where did this transformation come from?

Peter and John had been radically transformed by faith in Jesus through the power of the Holy Spirit. Recall that before His death on the cross, Jesus told His disciples that it was good that He was returning to the Father. Why? So that they could receive the permanent indwelling of the Holy Spirit. Jesus' words likely didn't make sense to His followers before His death, resurrection, and ascension. But here, after the coming of the Holy Spirit at Pentecost, the transformation that Jesus talked about was clear. Those who had been redeemed by faith in Christ would never be the same again.

We barely recognize the "Post-Pentecost Peter" as the same man as the "Pre-Pentecost Peter." I have been as guilty as anyone of comparing myself to Peter before the resurrection and the gift of the Holy Spirit because it's a much lower standard. This is a classic mistake we make far too many times. The standard by which we compare our lives should be their behavior after the resurrection and after they received the Holy Spirit.

We live under the banner of the complete fulfillment of God's plan for redemption. We have a full understanding of the crucifixion and resurrection. As the redeemed, we have received the Holy Spirit. Our standard for comparison is Peter and John as they are pictured in Acts 4, who are no longer afraid to be called disciples of Christ. Here, they tell the very same leaders they once feared that they could not stop talking about Jesus, and if they have to be punished because of their boldness, so be it. One thing is clear: Peter knows he will not betray or denounce Jesus again. He can't help but talk about Jesus.

One phrase we can't dodge is in vs. 13: "And they recognized that they had been with Jesus." The change in Peter and John was so obvious to these leaders. These weren't the same men they dealt with in the garden. I can almost imagine them saying to themselves, "Why aren't they running? Why don't they deny any association with Jesus? We are giving them an out; all they have to do is deny His power, and we won't punish them." And yet, Peter and John were unwavering.

Do people associate you with Jesus? Honestly, do you think the people who know you recognize that you have been in the presence of Jesus? Do you think that people who knew you when you were not a follower of Jesus would say you have been transformed into something that looks much different than the former you? Our goal should be that we are so connected to Jesus that our lives can't help but testify about Him.

FOR REFLECTION

After witnessing Jesus' crucifixion, resurrection, and ascension, and after receiving the Holy Spirit at Pentecost, Peter and John would never deny Jesus again. Their transformation through faith in Jesus was a game-changer. It raised the standard. We live on the other side of the resurrection. Has it changed you so much that your boldness and commitment to Christ cause all who encounter you to say that they recognize that you are with Jesus?

DAY 10
I NEVER KNEW YOU

"[21] Not everyone who says to me, 'Lord, Lord,' will enter the kingdom of Heaven, but the one who does the will of my Father who is in Heaven. [22] On that day many will say to me, 'Lord, Lord, did we not prophesy in your name, and cast out demons in your name, and do many mighty works in your name?' [23] And then will I declare to them, 'I never knew you; depart from me, you workers of lawlessness.'" -MATTHEW 7:21-23

Do these words from Jesus in Matthew 7 concern you? I can remember reading them and honestly being afraid that I might never have the assurance that I was truly redeemed. If you can relate to this feeling, hopefully, you can hear what Jesus is saying and what He isn't saying.

First, let's examine what has been going on leading up to this section of the Sermon on the Mount. Jesus has discussed false teachers and how to determine when a teacher is teaching false doctrine. Jesus tells us to look at the way they live their life. If we see them living a life or saying things that contradict the character or teachings of God, then they cannot be trusted. Jesus says that all of us eventually reveal who we are by how we live our lives. In Matthew 7:15-19 Jesus taught that false prophets or teachers are recognized by the fruit they bear; a healthy tree cannot bear bad fruit. Think about that: Jesus isn't saying that a healthy tree shouldn't bear bad fruit; He says a healthy tree cannot. Why? Because when we have truly been redeemed, the Spirit of God works through us to produce good fruit, i.e., righteousness. The Spirit at work in us is proof of our redemption.

Jesus says you will recognize my disciples by the fruit that they bear. Paul addresses this in Galatians 5 when he speaks of the fruit of the Spirit. God can't produce bad fruit. If our lives are defined by "bad fruit," i.e., patterns of sinfulness, then we have to question whether or not we have been transformed by saving faith in Jesus.

Now take that knowledge and look at our verses for today, where Jesus warns that there will be people who claim that He is their Lord. Paul tells us in Romans 10:9-10 that to come to saving faith in Jesus, we must confess with our mouths that

Jesus is Lord and believe in our hearts that God raised Him from the dead. Jesus says that people will say this with their mouths and even go as far as doing some works in His name. But the part He sees that we can't is the sincerity of the heart. God knows what a person truly believes. Therefore, Jesus tells us to look out for inconsistencies.

The part of these verses I missed for years is the second part of verse 21, where Jesus says we will recognize authentic Christ-followers by watching their lives to see if they are doing the will of the Father. I know many of us have been taught that if someone came forward in a service, said certain words, and got baptized by water, they were redeemed by Jesus and reconciled to a holy God. But it is not always that simple. The great evangelist Billy Sunday once had a large response of people come to the altar to make professions of faith after one of his sermons. A bystander was rightfully excited about the response. They asked Sunday to look at how many people were saved, to which Sunday replied, "we will see." The great evangelist knew what Jesus knew: the proof of their faith in Christ would be confirmed or revealed as false by the fruit their lives would bear moving forward.

Jesus said that many would claim to be His, but the ones who are truly transformed are obedient to the will of His Father. We must understand that obedience and legalism aren't the same things. I am concerned that in the modern Church's desire to remove legalism from the Church, we might have escorted obedience out the door. Legalism is no substitute for loving obedience. But we sometimes go too far under the good intentions of much-needed correction. Jesus says obedience to His commands proves our salvation and devotion to Him. Our lives tell the true story of our faith.

FOR REFLECTION

How do we measure up? Do you honestly see the fruit of the Holy Spirit in your life? What fruit is being produced in your life? Would people view your life and observe that your "Jesus as Lord" claim is authentic or just lip service?

DAY 11
THE FRUIT OF THE SPIRIT

"[22] But the fruit of the Spirit is love, joy, peace, patience, kindness, good-ness, faithfulness, [23] gentleness, self-control; against such things there is no law. [24] And those who belong to Christ Jesus have crucified the flesh with its passions and desires." -GALATIANS 5:22-24

Yesterday we briefly touched on Galatians 5 and what the Holy Spirit was direct-ing Paul to write to the churches in Galatia. The fruit of the Spirit is a list of nine characteristics (or attributes) that Paul says Christians are to exemplify. What does Paul mean when he describes this list of characteristics as the fruit of the Spirit? To better understand it, we might describe this list as the proof of the Spirit. These at-tributes are evidence of the Spirit's work in and through the lives of those who have been transformed. This is the work of the Holy Spirit, but there is another force at work that must be accounted for.

Paul writes that the Spirit and our flesh are at war. C.S. Lewis said that we could not truly understand the power of the flesh until we were redeemed and our flesh began to fight for its life. Lewis says that the one we feed is the one that wins. Be-fore you were redeemed, your fleshly desires ruled your life. If you have been truly redeemed, you know that a daily battle wages between the Spirit and your flesh.

If you look at the verses that proceed Galatians 5:22-24, you will find Paul instruct-ing us to walk by the Spirit. Paul tells us to walk by the Spirit so that we will not gratify the desires of the flesh. We find in the very next verse that Paul says the desires of the flesh are against the desires of the Spirit, and the desires of the Spirit are against the flesh. They stand in stark opposition to one other. Do you sense this war within yourself? Do you treat each day as another battle over who has control of your life?

Look at Galatians 5:19-21. Here we see a very clear warning from Paul. First, he lists things that are the works of the flesh. But he goes further. He warns us that those who do such things will not inherit the Kingdom of God. Leonard Ravenhill made a profound but sad statement about the modern Church when he said, "I think one of the tragedies of modern Christianity is this: that we are more afraid of holiness than we are of sinfulness. We can tolerate sin, but boy, we get our hackles up when you talk about holiness."

The Bible calls us to a transformed life that does not live enslaved to the desires of the flesh. Scripture universally condemns sin and elevates holiness. A Christian can't say we can be redeemed by the power that raised Jesus Christ from the dead and remain unchanged. If you believe this, you are saying we serve a God who can't transform us, which is an absurd statement. We must ask ourselves, therefore, "have we been transformed"?

Look at the list of the fruit of the Spirit and compare it to the list of the works of the flesh. Ask yourself a difficult question: "Which list looks more like your life"? Be honest. Have you ever considered that if you don't see the fruit of the Spirit in your life, it might be because you have not been transformed by saving faith in Jesus?

FOR REFLECTION

What needs to change in your life today? Look at the last line of today's passage: "And those who belong to Christ Jesus have crucified the flesh with its passions and desires." Maybe it's time for your flesh to be crucified. If so, do not wait a moment longer to do what you must do to be in right standing with God. Your very life may depend on it.

DAY 12
A GODLY LIFE

"His divine power has granted to us all things that pertain to life and godliness, through the knowledge of him who called us to his own glory and excellence." -2 PETER 1:3

I find it odd that men demand excellence from everything in their lives except their spiritual lives. Many men seem to hope that they have done enough to barely get into Heaven, which is good enough. Can I love you enough to warn you, brother, that if this is your game plan, you are placing your eternity on very dangerous theology?

Look at what Peter has to teach us. He says that God has allowed His divine power to be available to all who have been redeemed. Paul says something similar in Romans 8:15. Paul says we need to understand the spirit of adoption that has been extended to us by God's grace through saving faith in Jesus. Part of being transformed, Paul says, is that we are adopted into God's household. We are no longer slaves; we are children. This adoption gives us the right and privilege to call God "Father."

What is the spirit of this adoption? Picture a family who adopts a child into their home. Do you think this family would then limit access to the adopted child? Would the parents only allow the biological children their love and affection? Do you think the adopted child would somehow be viewed as a lower-level child by their parents? Of course not! Paul says our adoption into God's family is the same way. Because of the spirit of adoption, the redeemed can now call the great "I Am" our Father.

In Romans 8:16, Paul says that the Holy Spirit bears witness to us that we are indeed children of God and fellow heirs with Christ! But don't miss this very important detail in the latter part of Romans 8:17. This is all true "provided we suffer with him in order that we may be glorified with him." Peter echoes the same sentiment in 2 Peter 1:3, where he says that Jesus has called us to His glory and excellence.

Has your faith in Christ cost you anything? Paul tells Timothy in 2 Timothy 3:12 that all who choose to live a godly life will be persecuted. Peter tells us that Jesus' divine power has granted to us all that pertains to godliness through our knowledge of Him. According to Scripture, the option to remain in spiritual infancy isn't available to the children of God. Why? Because Jesus paved the way for a Holy power source for all the redeemed. This power enables us to live a godly life that inevitably brings persecution from the world.

Have you been persecuted at all due to your godliness? I examine my life and ask this question: does a lost and evil world find itself perfectly comfortable with my devotion to Christ? If yes, it is likely because I don't illuminate Him; I don't live a godly life.

Now let's ensure we're on the same page: Scripture doesn't teach us to go out looking for trouble. And it doesn't give us points for being "persecuted" because we're being self-righteous jerks. Scripture tells us that Jesus grants us access to a transformed life through His divine power that grows as we grow in our knowledge of Him.

FOR REFLECTION

Are you satisfied with what you know of God? I don't understand how any Christ-follower could answer that question with a "yes." Don't make the mistake of being spiritually complacent. Strive to know God more and better and start today. The more you know Him, the more you love Him, and the more you are loved by Him, the more you obey Him.

DAY 13

LIFE OR DEATH

"[12] So then, brothers, we are debtors, not to the flesh, to live according to the flesh. [13] For if you live according to the flesh you will die, but if by the Spirit you put to death the deeds of the body, you will live." -ROMANS 8:12-13

If you are still on this 31-day journey, you are picking up pretty quickly that Scripture cautions us of abusing God's grace. Sin always matters and should be taken extremely seriously. God hates sin so much that His son had to take His holy wrath on the cross to satisfy God's justice and pay the debt of our sins. How can we then take sin so lightly? The next time we decide to live in a way that seems to say that sin is no big deal, we should picture Jesus on the cross, bearing the wrath that was due us.

Have you ever been a little shocked by how many times you have heard people who claim to be redeemed talking like their life hasn't changed? Do they keep making the same mistakes? Sure, Paul tells us in Romans 7 that he still struggled with sin. As long as our flesh lives, we all will. However, as you discover, the disciple of Christ may struggle with his or her sinful nature, but the disciple of Christ does not live a life of sin. Paul is taking this on and reminding us that if we continue to live by the flesh, it will lead us to death. Paul encourages those who have been transformed by God to live by the Spirit because that leads to life.

In Jeremiah 21, we see a similar theme. Led by King Nebuchadnezzar, the Babylonians are about to besiege Judah, and God has told Jeremiah to tell the king of Judah and all who are in the great city to come out and surrender. God tells Jeremiah this message is a message of life or death. God told them to surrender to their enemies, and they would be captives, but they would live. God told them He would deliver them in His time. But if they chose to stay in the great city, they would die by the sword and be shown no mercy. God made it clear that the enemies of His people are not who they are fighting against. God said that due to their sin, He was now their enemy, and He was bringing the Babylonians against His people as discipline to bring them to repentance. His message to them was life or death.

Remember Romans 8:15 from yesterday. Recall Paul saying that we haven't received from Christ a spirit of slavery to sin. Paul is urging us not to fall back to fear. In other words, don't fall back to the former life. If you are in Jesus, you are living your new life in Christ. We must leave the city of sin and surrender to the bondage of our Lord and Savior, Jesus Christ. To stay in our sin is death. But to leave our sin and be taken as a bondservant to Christ Is life.

FOR REFLECTION

Where do you find yourself? Do you continue to hunker down in your city of sin? Are there sins you just refuse to leave? Jesus stands ready and able to transform all who are willing to repent and stop living according to the flesh. He makes it possible to live by the Spirit, which is life. But the first step is surrendering the sinful habits we bind ourselves to. Is today the day in which you do that? Isn't it time?

DAY 14
GOD'S WORKMANSHIP

"[8] For by grace you have been saved through faith. And this is not your own doing; it is the gift of God, [9] not a result of works, so that no one may boast. [10] For we are his workmanship, created in Christ Jesus for good works, which God prepared beforehand, that we should walk in them."
-EPHESIANS 2:8-10

Inspired by the Holy Spirit, the Apostle Paul writes in Ephesians 2:8-10 that we are redeemed by God's grace alone through our faith in Christ alone. We can do no work on our own to redeem ourselves. We can never live a life good enough to accomplish the standard of perfection required by a perfect and holy God. This is not up for debate. Paul makes this crystal clear. Paul was addressing a "works-based" way of thinking about salvation that had entered the Church. This works-based notion wasn't biblically sound.

We call this works-based approach "legalism." Legalism says that we can earn our salvation by following God's rules or commands. It's a good thing that, by and large, the Church recognizes that legalism is no way to approach our faith. But sometimes, I wonder if we've swung the pendulum too far in the other direction.

I am sure you have heard people say, "You don't have to be perfect to get into heaven!" The only problem with this statement is that it's 100% incorrect. The standard required to stand in the presence of the living, holy, and perfect God is perfection. We must be fully righteous, not partially righteous. Only the perfect can stand before God. Period. That's why the Gospel is good news! The Gospel message is that Jesus, the Son of God, came to earth to live a perfect life and die on the cross as a once-and-for-all perfect sacrifice to pay the penalty for the sins of humankind. When we repent of our sins and profess faith in Jesus, God, in His grace, allows Jesus' sacrifice to count on our behalf. In that way, Jesus purchases our righteousness. Paul says in Romans 8:4 that Jesus has satisfied the righteous requirements of the Law on our behalf. And to be seen as righteous in God's eyes and as perfect, we simply need to submit in faith to the lordship of the Son of

God. That is the pathway to salvation and transformation. We cannot do any of this for ourselves, no matter how "good" we try to be. Only Jesus presents us as fully righteous, reconciling us to our Holy Father. God did for us what we could not do for ourselves.

Most of you are probably thinking, "I already know this. And why is this being covered in a devotional about transformation?" The answer is found in verse 10: "For we are his workmanship, created in Christ Jesus for good works, which God prepared beforehand, that we should walk in them." The Holy Spirit led Paul to remind the Church that though works don't earn us salvation, they are the result of salvation. Moreso, God has prepared works for us that He expects us to do now that we are new creations in Christ Jesus.

Sadly, we don't hear as much about verse 10 as we do about verses 8 and 9. My concern is that in the correct desire to remove legalism from the Church, we've also thrown out obedience. The problem with this is that it isn't biblical. The Bible teaches that a day is coming when the redeemed will stand before the judgment seat and will be judged by the works or lack of works done after our redemption (2 Corinthians 5:10). Jesus says in John 14 that those who love Him show their love through their obedience.

Praise God that He has made a way in Christ to transform us from dead sinners to living sons and daughters. But in our haste to lean on the grace of God, let's not forget the expectation God has for us. The transformed life is a life of obedience that leads to the good works God has prepared in advance.

FOR REFLECTION

The questions we must ask ourselves today are these: Do I see evidence in my transformed life of works for the Kingdom of God? If I were to face Jesus today before the judgment seat, would I be able to say that I pursued obedience out of love for God? Is there at least one person that I have reached and discipled?

DAY 15

GOD'S CHILDREN

"[1] See what kind of love the Father has given to us, that we should be called children of God; and so we are. The reason why the world does not know us is that it did not know him. [2] Beloved, we are God's children now, and what we will be has not yet appeared; but we know that when he appears we shall be like him, because we shall see him as he is. [3] And everyone who thus hopes in him purifies himself as he is pure." - 1 JOHN 3:1-3

I have parents I respect, and many times in my childhood, I corrected my behavior because I did not want to embarrass and disrespect their names. You can understand that motivation whether you have parents you respect or not. In our Scripture today, John is writing to a church struggling with false theology that has crept into the congregation. The Gnostics claimed that Jesus could not have been 100% man and 100% God and never have committed a sin. Their teaching was that the flesh is sinful; therefore, Jesus could not have taken on flesh and remained sinless. The takeaway from this false teaching was that God is OK with sin because it comes with being a human. Don't take your sin so seriously. It's not a big deal. (This is similar to the modern Universalists who falsely teach that God is only love and grace, so everyone is going to Heaven.)

Into this atmosphere of false teaching, John reminds the Church in chapter 1 that he was a first-hand witness to the person and teaching of Christ. John reminded them that he touched Jesus' flesh, implying (rightfully so) that he is a much more reliable source. John makes the case that since God's grace has made us His children, we should prepare to face Him by striving to live pure lives and not embracing sin as something that can't be overcome.

In verse 5, John says that no one who abides in God keeps sinning. John says if we are truly in Christ, then the power of God is now in us; due to that power, we can't just keep on sinning. Look at verses 9-10. John says no one (not some but none) born of God makes the practice of sinning, for God's seed abides in him, and he cannot keep on sinning because he has been born of God. Wow! John said that if

God is your perfect father and you are His child, then due to the power of your father's seed that has rejuvenated your dead spirit and brought it back to life, you can't live a lifestyle or a pattern of deliberate sin anymore. Sin might be perfectly comfortable to your dead flesh but not your new spirit. God is too powerful.

John drives this point home in verse 24. Whoever keeps God's commandments abides in God and God in him. How do we know that God abides in us? By the Spirit He has given us. Do you hear what John is saying? You may still struggle with your sinful desire while being sanctified, and that struggle will be there until you are glorified. But the person you were before God's seed made you His child should be gone.

When the Holy Spirit comes into our dead spirit, we are transformed. When we stumble, we feel the displeasure of our holy Father, who hates sin. This is conviction. And because of our love for God, we strive anew to resist temptation and pursue holiness. This is the relationship with sin we should all have as those who God has transformed.

FOR REFLECTION

Are you aware of God's conviction when it comes to your sin? Has the power of God making you His child caused you to see sin differently? Or are you comfortable with sin? John says to pursue holiness in preparation for meeting your perfect father. Do you live your life in such a way that you are anticipating the Lord's return?

DAY 16

SANCTIFIED

"[3] For this is the will of God, your sanctification . . . [7] For God has not called us for impurity, but in holiness." -1 THESSALONIANS 4:3a, 7

On Day 10 of this devotional, you read Matthew 7:21, where Jesus told His followers that many people would use His name and claim to be with Him. But He warned us that only those who do the will of the Father would inherit the Kingdom of Heaven. In 1 Thessalonians 4, Paul tells the Church at Thessalonica that though he is hearing good things about them, they should commit to their ongoing sanctification. Paul says that our sanctification is the will of God. Don't miss this point. Jesus says that only those who do His father's will are truly His disciples. Paul says the Father's will is our sanctification. Surely there are other things God desires for us; His will is not only our sanctification. But when we look at the words of Scripture from Jesus to Paul and all in between, we are left with a clear expectation that the transformed would be sanctified.

What is sanctification? To be sanctified is to be made holy. It is both an event and a process. When we come to saving faith in the person and work of Jesus, we are at once sanctified in God's eyes. At that moment, we are born-again of the Spirit. We are transformed. We are "new creations," as Paul says in 2 Corinthians 5:17, and God sees us as holy, not because of anything we've done for ourselves but because of the imparted righteousness of Christ on our behalf. In His grace, God sees us through the sacrifice of Christ. He does not see our sin. He sees the righteousness that Jesus purchased for us. We are at once sanctified. But it doesn't stop there.

As you and I both know, even though God sees us as holy because of what Jesus did for us on the cross, we still struggle with a sinful nature. So while we are sanctified in God's eyes, we must still begin a process of sanctification where we partner with the Holy Spirit to live a Christ-like life, day in and day out. We resist temptation and pursue holiness. This is the process aspect of sanctification, the leaving behind of our spiritual infancy and moving forward toward spiritual maturity.

For anyone claiming to be transformed, this process must take place. Brother, you must be taking deliberate action to grow spiritually. So are you? While the process of sanctification covers every aspect of our lives, notice that Paul uses sexual purity as a marker for sanctification. Paul says those who are being sanctified know how to control their bodies. Paul says the disciple of Christ is not called to impurity but is called to holiness.

Paul tells the Church in Corinth to run away from sexual immorality, to flee from it (1 Corinthians 6:18)! Why? Because Paul knew what you and I see all around us: The Adversary uses the sin of sexual immorality to destroy more men than seemingly any other sin. Therefore Paul says, don't be a sin daredevil when it comes to sexual immorality! If we're brutally honest, sexual immorality has destroyed men much stronger than us; why would we think we can stand toe-to-toe with it and remain pure?

The prudent response for the man who wants to remain undamaged by the sin of sexual immorality is to take action. Go the other way. But we must be vigilant. Everywhere we go in this fallen creation, something is trying to draw us into its allure. We must stop playing games by letting our eyes wander, and our minds drift. If a woman chooses to be immodest, don't applaud that behavior. One day that may be your daughter who saw her father behave in a way that taught her to compromise her purity to win a man's affection. Don't teach her that lesson by your lack of control over sexual sin.

I never saw victory in this area until I began to flee from sexual sin and run to Jesus. I take my eyes off the temptation of the world and put my eyes on Jesus. I don't seek pleasure outside of my wife and my devotion to Christ. I cannot compromise my union with the wife God gave me. My goal is to find total satisfaction in God by seeking and immersing myself in Jesus to the point that I love Him more than I love sin. How silly to think anything else can satisfy me so fully.

FOR REFLECTION

Are you ready to repent of your sexual sin today? Until you do, you can never be the man that only God can make you. Are you seeking Jesus? Do you know Him so personally that nothing else quite draws you like Him? Let's commit that we will no longer behave like those who do not know Him.

There has never been a faithful follower of Christ who gave sexual immorality free reign. Do what it takes today to redouble your efforts in this area of sanctification.

DAY 17
LIFE IN THE SPIRIT

"[16] But I say, walk by the Spirit, and you will not gratify the desires of the flesh. [17] For the desires of the flesh are against the Spirit, and the desires of the Spirit are against the flesh, for these are opposed to each other, to keep you from doing the things you want to do." -GALATIANS 5:16–17

C.S. Lewis once said that you couldn't understand the power of the Nazis by going along with them; to truly understand the power of the Nazis, you had to oppose them. This is the same with the flesh.

Before your faith in Jesus transformed you, the flesh had no opponent. Due to the sinful nature humankind has inherited because of the Fall, you live with a sinful desire. We call this the flesh. But when you repented of your sin and surrendered your life's authority to the lordship of Jesus Christ, God's grace paved the way for the Spirit to come alive within you. When this happens, the flesh begins to fight for its life. Have you found this to be true?

If you are redeemed and desire to follow Jesus, war wages inside you between the Spirit and the flesh. The one you feed is the one who will win. I have found in my own life that when I respond to anything from the flesh, I am always wrong. We must learn to respond through the Spirit, not the flesh. The flesh is dying. But if we've been saved by faith in Christ, we've embraced a life fueled by the Spirit.

Over the years, as I've done risky things, I've had people warn me: "Be careful because you just might die," or "What's going to happen to you if you die"? Of course, we must always be prepared to die. But maybe even more importantly, we need to be prepared to live.

We need to be ready to die for our faith, but we must put even more effort into living out our faith. Yes, I will die for my wife, but will I live for my wife? Yes, I would die for my children, but will I live for my children? Jesus didn't just die for me; He lives for me. To those saved by faith, He promises the Holy Spirit. We were dead in our sins, but now we are alive in Christ. So why are we feeding the part of us that is dying as opposed to the part that is living? Watch what you are doing, not because you might die but because you might live. It's while we are living that we do the most good or the most damage. Feed the Spirit, not the flesh.

A good example of this in my own life has to do with praise and worship music. When I was first transformed, I still loved secular music (mainly rock) much more than praise and worship music. I decided to legalistically make myself listen to praise and worship, not because I desired the music over secular music, but because I thought this was what I should do to earn God's approval. I quickly discovered that this didn't work, and it frustrated me so much that I just stopped trying.

Then, over time, I fell in love with Scripture. I began to listen to Bible studies, take notes during church, spend time in prayer, and so on. Something happened as my spirit was being fed regularly. I got in the car one day (it was back when we had the 6-disc changers, and you could load 6 CDs at one time), and I noticed that the first CD was praise and worship music. And so were the second, third, and fifth. Just a few months before this, they were all secular music. I had been feeding my flesh, but now that I was feeding the Spirit, I began to hunger for something different.

The Spirit was and is winning the war being waged inside me. I do not accomplish this by a new set of rules, or some new self-control. I accomplish this because I partner with the Spirit, "feeding" the Spirit and starving my flesh.

FOR REFLECTION

The flesh and the Spirit are opposed to each other. They are not friends. Do you hear that? One leads to death, and the other to life. Which one are you feeding? Whatever you have to do, stop feeding your flesh. Stop doing things that lead you to embrace your sinful nature, and instead, surround yourself with godly things. Starve the desire in you that wants to pursue sinfulness.

DAY 18
THE MARKS OF JESUS

"From now on let no one cause me trouble, for I bear on my body the marks of Jesus." -GALATIANS 6:17

Paul is writing to the churches of Galatia who have started to desert the sound theology they had been taught. One issue was that many new Jewish converts, called Judaizers, were teaching that circumcision was needed for salvation. Paul makes it crystal clear that even those who had been physically circumcised still didn't keep all the Law (vs. 13). Furthermore, Paul pointed out that one of the reasons the Judaizers wanted people to get circumcised was so that they would be more like themselves. Paul went on to say that the only "mark" that identified him was the mark of God's grace, the cross of our Lord, Jesus Christ (vs. 14).

Do you bear the marks of Jesus? As we have arrived at day 18 of this 31-day journey, you should have picked up on a running theme by now. Those who have truly had an encounter with Jesus Christ bear His marks. The only thing good about any of us who have been transformed by faith in Christ is Jesus; we bring nothing to the table.

I love that Paul says that he is tired of anyone continuing to cause him trouble over the ridiculous argument about circumcision. He says that the grace of God has redeemed him, and that is the mark he bears.

What marks do you bear? If I were to ask that question to those closest to you, how would they answer? There are many marks of Jesus. Love. Steadfastness. Sacrifice. Mercy. Faithfulness. Commitment. And many more. Forgiveness would certainly be near the top of the list, wouldn't it? How are you doing in the forgiveness department? For many of us, that's a tough question.

God has forgiven us in Christ. He has forgiven us much. So why would we deny forgiveness to people that Jesus did not deny us? Now let me be clear: forgiving someone for what they did to you doesn't mean what they did is OK or that it doesn't matter. But to deny forgiveness to others isn't bearing a mark of Jesus. Being ungraceful is going against the heart of God.

Unforgiveness can cause bitterness to creep into our lives, which can become a cancer. But the ultimate reason we forgive those who mistreat us is that Jesus did. We claim that we belong to Jesus; He purchased us on the cross, and we now submit to Him as our Lord. He said to forgive people, so that's what we do. To withhold forgiveness is to sin against God. Bottom line.

FOR REFLECTION

Don't you think it's time to be obedient to the one you belong to, forgive these people who have harmed you, and move on with your sanctification? How much longer will you harbor this bitterness and resentment that only hurts you and keeps you from being a more powerful man of God? Stop letting others cause you trouble because now you bear the marks of Jesus.

DAY 19
CEASING TO SIN

"[1] Since therefore Christ suffered in the flesh, arm yourselves with the same way of thinking, for whoever has suffered in the flesh has ceased from sin, [2] so as to live for the rest of the time in the flesh no longer for human passions but for the will of God." -1 PETER 4:1-2

These verses of the Holy Bible grace the refrigerator in a little white farmhouse on some land the Lord blessed us with in 2007. We got this little farm only three months before our youngest son died tragically. We mourned at that farm for months, and as God was refining us through our suffering, my wife began to search Scripture for every word that God had spoken on the subject of suffering. She put it all together in a book called *"Bronner* (our son's name): *A Journey to Understand."*

During our time at the farm, Sherri wrote these verses on paper and put them on the refrigerator door. It is still there today. It is faded, but it remains there to remind us of these Holy Spirit-inspired words written by Peter during a time of incredible suffering. The emperor Nero had begun a season of horrific persecution of Christians. Peter reminded the church that Christ suffered in the flesh, so as His disciples, we should arm ourselves with the same thinking.

What is the same way of thinking? To remember why Jesus suffered in the flesh. He suffered in the flesh to defeat sin. He was offering us redemption and victory over sin, which, apart from Him, leads us to death. Peter is telling the church, as the persecution was at the door, to remember to use this suffering not to give in to sin and deny Jesus but to embrace the suffering to glorify Jesus.

Living for the glory of God despite great trials is the true call of the transformed. May His will be done, not ours! For example, when sexual temptations come, we do not give in because we will live for and by the will of God. Those being transformed by their sufferings are being refined, and their sinful nature is being destroyed because they are no longer a slave to their dying flesh. The worst thing that could happen concerning suffering is to experience it and not be changed.

Part of how we understand God allowing suffering in the world is understanding that God uses suffering to purify us, refining us in the fire of trials to destroy the sin in our lives, draw us closer to Him, and provide us a platform to bring Him glory. Let your suffering change you, not destroy you. When we see suffering as part of how God grows our faith, it gives us a perspective the world cannot understand. Those who have been transformed by faith are continually transformed. Many times this transformation happens in the furnace. It isn't easy, but when we come out refined on the other side, we accept that it is necessary and, in the end, glorifying to God.

FOR REFLECTION

What is your posture in suffering? When you have gone through a trial, do you blame God? Is His power diminished in your sight? Are you tempted to doubt His character? While God is big enough to handle all our emotions, and our raw hurt does not offend or turn Him away, our posture in suffering must be, "teach me, Lord." If you find yourself in the midst of suffering, how are you doing with glorifying God through this trial? If you are not in a period of suffering, what can you do to prepare yourself for the next time it comes?

DAY 20

BE HOLY

"[13] Therefore, preparing your minds for action, and being sober-minded, set your hope fully on the grace that will be brought to you at the revelation of Jesus Christ. [14] As obedient children, do not be conformed to the passions of your former ignorance, [15] but as he who called you is holy, you also be holy in all your conduct, [16] since it is written, 'You shall be holy, for I am holy.'" -1 PETER 1:13-16

As you read today's verses, I sense that you may have noticed some verbiage that challenged you a little. We have discussed holiness in many of our resources at themanchurch.com, and we will continue to do so because it's a topic that gets so much pushback. Why are people so uncomfortable with holiness? The standard of holiness should only make you uncomfortable or discouraged if you have the notion that your power somehow achieves this.

We read these verses on holiness, and it seems so unattainable that we miss the point that holiness doesn't come from us but from the power of God in us. We act like God has called us to a standard He can't achieve. We don't like looking at these verses and reading that Peter is reminding us that we are not called to be holy in some of our conduct but in all of our conduct. All of our conduct? Yes, all of our conduct. I do a pretty good job of being holy in some of my conduct, but I am still working toward the goal of being holy in all of my conduct. Let's break down the verses, so we don't miss the challenge to work toward this goal in Christ.

We are told to prepare our minds for action, to be sober-minded, and to set our hope on what is to come when Christ glorifies us, declaring the battle with the flesh is over. We should be men of action. We should not just let our minds wander; we should take action to focus and think about holy things. We should be sober-minded, meaning we should be fully aware of our need for God's grace, and we should not let anything alter our minds to keep us from thinking clearly. Have you noticed that people behave differently when they are not sober? If we are not sober-minded, we lack the intentionality it takes to pursue a Christ-centered life.

Next, Peter tells us to be obedient children because we can no longer claim ignorance regarding sin. He calls the behavior of our old self "ignorant." We can no longer be conformed to the old self; that person should be dead. I even use the phrase old Rick and new Rick. I don't let old Rick tell new Rick how to act anymore. I am not ignorant of the problems my past life caused me. Why would I go back and do the same things that caused me problems before? If behavior causes you issues at any time, it will cause you issues every time. Peter says we can't live like we don't know right from wrong anymore.

Then Peter says, like the God we serve is holy, we should also be holy in all our conduct. How? The ongoing grind of sanctification. If you and I are willing to immerse ourselves in the power of our holy God - seeking Him, loving Him with all our heart, soul, strength, and mind - He will make us holy just like Him. Do you believe that?

FOR REFLECTION

God is indeed the driver of our holiness. We cannot be holy apart from the work of the Spirit in us. But let me ask: are there trouble spots in your life that consistently trip you up? Do you struggle with anger, gossip, or a critical spirit? Do you struggle with lustful thoughts or sexual temptation? Do you have a hard time tempering your appetite for food or alcohol? If you have areas of your life that you know are trouble spots, why not focus on addressing these areas head-on? What can you do today to minimize the impact of your specific weakness on your holiness? Maybe it's talking to someone. Maybe it's not going certain places. Maybe it's not being with certain people. Whatever it is, do the work today to take steps toward addressing your weak spots. And do so in the knowledge that you're not alone.

DAY 21

A DEMONIC FAITH

"You believe that God is one; you do well. Even the demons believe—and shudder!" - JAMES 2:19

The book of James can be very difficult. James was the earthly brother of Jesus and, early in his life, did not believe his brother's claim about being the Son of God. It was not until after the resurrection that James believed that his earthly brother might have had the same mother as him but was God's Son.

Out of this new belief, James took on the difficult job of shepherding the first church in Jerusalem. James writes this letter to the church and begins to point out the sins of the church members and how their behavior was inconsistent with their claim to be Christ-followers. In chapter 2, James takes on a topic that remains controversial to this very day: do works matter?

James begins to discuss the topic of saving faith. James would agree with Paul that we are saved by grace through faith alone. James saw his brother alive after the resurrection and knows first-hand the power of the Holy Spirit because He raised his brother from the dead. Based on his understanding of the transformative power of the Holy Spirit, James asks how anyone can claim to have a saving faith and be indifferent toward obeying the commandments of the Lord they claim to serve.

James then brings up the question of belief. What sort of belief do we have? James says in verse 19 that if we just accept the historical facts of Jesus but do not truly believe, we are no different than the demons. That's a bold statement. But James correctly points out that the demons know who Jesus is and acknowledge that He is the Son of God. We must look to Scripture and see that the demons knew exactly who Jesus was, even when the disciples didn't yet fully understand. In Matthew 8:29, they call Him the Son of God. In Luke 4:41, we see that the demons knew Jesus was the Christ. In Acts 19:15, the demon says that he knows who Jesus is. The demons know Jesus. Do you?

James warns us that if all our "belief" in Jesus is just historical and factual, then we may have a problem. James goes on to suggest the best way to see if we have a saving faith or a demonic faith is to look at the evidence of obedience in our lives. James clearly states that our righteous deeds, our godly works, do not earn our salvation. They are not how we are saved. James says that our righteous works are the evidence of saving faith. We are not Christians because of our good works. But if we do not have good works, we must ask, "are we Christians?"

FOR REFLECTION

Which faith do you have? The demons believed that Jesus was who He said He was, but they rebelled against Him. The disciple of Jesus believes that Jesus is who He says He is and then turns from rebellion, submits to the authority of Christ, and places all his faith in Him. The power of God then produces in him the works that confirm that proclamation. So which faith best describes your life right now? Demonic faith or saving faith?

DAY 22

NOT IN VAIN

"[9] For I am the least of the apostles, unworthy to be called an apostle, because I persecuted the church of God. [10] But by the grace of God I am what I am, and his grace toward me was not in vain. On the contrary, I worked harder than any of them, though it was not I, but the grace of God that is with me." -1 CORINTHIANS 15:9-10

What humility Paul is showing in today's verses. Here is a man who wrote more of the New Testament than anyone else and had the humility to declare that he was not even worthy to be called an apostle. He says he is the least of the apostles. Why?

First, we know that Paul's claim to be an apostle was a bone of contention with some of the original disciples. Paul continually defended this title due to his encounter with the glorified Jesus on the road to Damascus. Due to this encounter, Paul was rightfully declared an apostle. But there was another issue that burdened Paul.

Paul was mindful of his former persecution of the Church he was advancing. If you look back at the stoning of Stephen in Acts 7, Luke informs us in verse 58 that those who were stoning Stephen placed their garments at the feet of a young man named Saul, who we, of course, know is Paul. Why did they need to remove garments? The answer is so they could throw harder and more accurately at the person they were stoning. Acts 8:1 tells us that Paul approved of the execution of Stephen. Paul saw this man full of faith, power, and the Holy Spirit die. And as Stephen dies, Paul hears Stephen say, "Lord, do not hold this sin against them." Do you think he ever forgot that encounter? Apparently not.

Paul says he's unworthy to be called an apostle because he persecuted the church. In light of his past, he worked harder than the others to show his integrity and to testify with his life that he had become a champion of the Church. He advanced the Gospel with more zeal than he had when persecuting the Church. Paul had been completely transformed. But don't miss what he says about the grace of God.

Paul is clear that the only thing good about him is Jesus. He says so humbly and correctly that the only way he could be of any value to the Church was due to the grace of God.

But don't miss the next point. Paul says he has committed his life to Christ to such an extent that God would never look at the life of Paul and consider the grace He poured out to be in vain. What an incredible motivation for living out our faith.

How about you? Are you living your life in such a way in response to God's grace that He would never consider His grace to be wasted on you? Is God getting a return on the grace He has afforded us? I see the former sin in my life not as a weapon to be used against me by the adversary, but as a reminder of just how gracious God has been, now and then. If you struggle with your past, I'd advise you to have the same focus.

FOR REFLECTION

Respond to God as an obedient child, committing to live in a way that says to your gracious Father, "Thank you. Thank you, Father, for the grace you have shown me. I'll be more faithful because I know how much I have been forgiven. Thank you." Have you thanked your gracious Father? Maybe today is the time to do so.

DAY 23
BORN OF GOD

"No one born of God makes a practice of sinning, for God's seed abides in him; and he cannot keep on sinning, because he has been born of God."
- 1 JOHN 3:9

Nicodemus was a member of the Jewish religious elite. He approached Jesus with questions to try to vet Him out over the claim Jesus was making that He was the Son of God. Jesus told Nicodemus that unless one is born again, he cannot see the Kingdom of God (John 3:3). Years later, see how John echoed Jesus' words. In his epistle, John states that no one born of God makes a practice of sinning. But he then explains why this is true.

John knows what Jesus knew: when we come to saving faith in Jesus, we're transformed, and a rebirth has occurred. God is now within us, and we cannot keep on sinning due to the presence and power of the Holy Spirit in our lives. We have been born of God. It is truly a new birth.

Now, this wasn't and isn't a teaching that makes everyone feel super-comfortable. We have already discussed in this devotion that John was taking on the false theology that was rampant in the early Church that sin was no big deal; as long as you have flesh, it's impossible not to sin. These were the teachings of the Gnostics, and they went as far as to say Jesus could not have been 100% man and 100% God due to the fact he had taken on flesh. John takes this false theology on by reminding the Church that he heard the teachings of Christ first-hand, both before and after the resurrection. He recalled Jesus teaching about the new birth that we all must have to stand in the presence of a perfect and holy God.

Don't miss the word abide used by John in these verses. What does it mean to abide in something? It means to decide to remain, act in accordance with, or immerse yourself in something. John says that the new birth comes from God's seed abiding in us once we are redeemed. Remember, our sinful nature comes from the seed of Adam, which is why Jesus was born of a virgin and has a perfect and holy Father. When we are transformed, God's seed replaces Adam's seed. Our sinful nature should no longer rule us.

Do we have the power not to sin? Scripture surely says that we do. Paul says in Romans 6:6 that when we come to saving faith in Jesus, we are no longer slaves to sin. We are freed from sin's power over us. But if you listen to much of what passes for Christian thought these days, you might think that redemption doesn't change our sinful nature, only that we are forgiven. But that's not what John says here at all.

John says that God's seed abides in the redeemed, and due to that power, we no longer practice sinning. To stumble is one thing; we will never be free from sin until we're glorified in heaven with God. But perpetual, deliberate sin is problematic. John is not saying we cannot sin, but we have been given the power to choose not to sin. We may still choose to sin, but we at least have the choice in Christ. Before we were redeemed, our spirit was dead, so we had no power over sin. When we are transformed, our spirit goes from dead to alive. Does your life look like you are accessing God's power over sin? Or are you simply disregarding it so you can continue making excuses for your sin? It's a powerful question worth asking today.

FOR REFLECTION

Why would you make excuses, ignoring the power of God and attempting to justify your sin? Maybe because you still love some sin more than you love God? That may be a very direct way of saying that, but it's true, isn't it? If we don't stop our perpetual sin, aren't we saying that we love that sin more than we love God? We must understand today that if we continue to practice sin, it is not because we have no power over its enticement. We are choosing it over the power God provides to those who have been born again.

DAY 24
PUTTING OFF THE OLD SELF

"[9] Do not lie to one another, seeing that you have put off the old self with its practices [10] and have put on the new self, which is being re-newed in knowledge after the image of its creator." -COLOSSIANS 3:9-10

My weight has been something I have struggled with for most of my life. I started taking it seriously, and instead of overeating and refusing to exercise, I began to eat healthier and became much more physically active. I am the type of man who needs accountability, so I surrounded myself with trainers who would watch my nutrition and oversee my workout strategy. As part of that strategy, I began to use the phrase Paul uses here in his letter to the Colossians.

Paul talks about the "new self vs. the old self." Notice Paul doesn't treat this analogy in a passive way. No, he instructs the Colossians to put off the old self and put on the new self! This command is an active one. We must take action to grow spiritually and develop new habits while throwing away the old ones that were part of our old selves.

My trainers picked up on this language. They would say things to me to encourage me when they'd give me that day's workout. They'd say things like, "Old Rick would have skipped this workout," or "Old Rick would not have passed on that ice cream like new Rick did today," and so on. It was the proper analogy for my fitness situation, and it's the proper analogy for your walk in Christ.

Paul says the sanctification process is ultimately us being renewed in the knowledge of the image of God. I can't claim to be ignorant about God if I actively throw off the old self and put on the new self. This also means there is an expectation of the new self and the new behaviors and attitudes that go with it. The practices of the old self should be dying and the new practices and habits of the new self should be different, as they are corrections of the practices and habits of the old self.

Walk this out with me: How do we know which practices belong to which self? Through the ongoing knowledge of the God who redeemed us. Haven't you changed some of your behavior after discovering more about God? Haven't you stopped doing things you thought were OK at one time because you didn't know any better? That is the caution; if you don't actively put off the old self and actively put on the new self, you may remain in ignorance. But that will not be an adequate excuse when we stand before God. Why? Because He has provided the answers that we need but must seek them.

In Jeremiah 29:13, we see something so simple yet so profound. God says that if we seek Him, we will find Him if we seek Him with all of our hearts. Do you hear that? If we have not found God and do not know God in such a way that we are putting on our new self, it is because we have not sought Him with all of our hearts.

God promises that if we sincerely seek Him, we will find Him. Period. Notice that Paul gives us a marker when he uses the example of the old self. Paul says do not lie to one another. Paul says one indicator of our old self is lying. Jesus says in John 8 that when we lie, we are speaking the native language of Satan because he is the father of lies. Paul says one step to removing the old self is to stop lying and take the truth very seriously. Jesus says He is "the way, the truth, and the life" (John 14:6), so the question is whether we speak the native language of Satan or Jesus. What about you? Are you walking around in the dead ways of your old self or the powerful truth of the new self?

FOR REFLECTION

Have you gotten lazy and lost your desire to continue to put off your old self and put on your new self? Don't forget that the old self was leading us to eternal death, while the new self sanctifies us into eternal life. What do you need to throw out of your life that represents the old? Whatever it is, put it off. Stop listening to the old self.

DAY 25
FREE FROM SIN

"[1] What shall we say then? Are we to continue in sin that grace may abound? [2] By no means! How can we who died to sin still live in it?"
- ROMANS 6:1-2

This devotional is full of verses that greatly challenge us. Romans chapter 6 takes on the issue of "grace abuse" as clearly as anywhere in the Bible. Paul can't believe that anyone is suggesting that just because they have been saved by the grace of God and not by their abilities, they can continue to sin and show how gracious God can be. Paul is astonished at this notion. When Paul says, "by no means" (or "certainly not" as some translations say), the original Greek being used here is intense.

Paul is offended by the thought that we would know the sacrifice of Christ on the cross and the suffering He endured to merely say, "thanks for grace, Jesus, but I think I will just keep on doing what I've always done just show everyone how gracious you are." The notion was as absurd to Paul's ears as it should be to ours. Listen to me and listen very clearly: if your game plan is to ask for God's forgiveness, then enjoy all of the world's pleasures, hoping you have "believed' enough things and said the right prayer in hopes that you have done the bare minimum to still get into heaven, then, my friend, you are playing a very dangerous game.

Paul asks how anyone who has truly died to sin can still live in it. I have had men tell me they were saved by faith but still watch filthy movies and listen to obscene music, then try to convince me that because they are redeemed, it doesn't bother them. But here is the problem: it should! That's the point Paul is making. God hates sin. Therefore, if we have been transformed, we died to sin, and now we are disgusted by sin due to the Holy Spirit abiding inside us.

Look at verse 6. Here Paul says that we know our old self was crucified with Jesus so that the body of sin might be brought to nothing so that we would no longer be enslaved to sin. Verse 7 says that one who has died has been set free from sin! Verse 11 challenges us to consider yourselves dead to sin and alive to God in Christ Jesus. Paul says that before our redemption, we were slaves to sin, but when Jesus redeems us, we become slaves to righteousness. We have been set from the slavery of sin. What an incredible truth.

Do you know what this means, brother? This means that if we go back to sin now, we go back as free men. We choose to return to that garbage after being freed from the dump. It's the drug addict who leaves rehab clean and returns to the drugs until the drugs kill them. Verse 17 makes it clear we were once slaves to sin, but now we have become obedient from the heart to the standard of teaching to which we have committed. Set free from sin, now a slave to righteousness. If that is true then sin should make us sick. Does it? Does your sin make you sick?

FOR REFLECTION

Do you realize what your sin cost God? Sin always matters, and it always damages. What has your redemption cost you? It should have cost us our sin. Today, give yourself some time to think about the cost of your redemption. Marinate on it. Consider it, in hopes that it motivates you to live a more godly life.

DAY 26
THE FOUNDATION

"[24] Everyone then who hears these words of mine and does them will be like a wise man who built his house on the rock. [25] And the rain fell, and the floods came, and the winds blew and beat on that house, but it did not fall, because it had been founded on the rock."
-MATTHEW 7:24-25

Today I want to ask you a very tough question: "What foundation is your life built upon"? I do not want you to answer the question with the answer that you think you should say. I want you to be honest with yourself. Jesus makes it very clear how to correctly define the foundation on which our lives currently rest. The question is, are you following His commands?

Jesus said that we will build our foundation on a rock if we are wise. This rock is God's Word. The life built on the rock is defined as a person who hears the words of God and does them. So, the first thing we have to get right to have the proper foundation is hearing or knowing the Bible.

This book is a good resource, but building the right foundation will require more than a 31-day devotional. It will require us intentionally putting together a game plan to become an expert on the Word of God. What sort of game plan? How about we devote the same time and passion to our spiritual maturation as we do to everything else we deem of value? Just work the same plan.

Then next thing Jesus demands is for us to do what He says. It's one thing to hear it and quite another to follow those words and put them into action. Let's notice that Jesus says that even those willing to be wise and build their house on the proper foundation will still face rain, floods, and heavy winds. Don't miss this very crucial point. The storms came against both houses, not just the foolish man who hears the words of Jesus and does not do them. The wise man faces the same storms, but the difference is that he and his house survive the storms because they are in Christ. Which man are you? It's very simple to determine which man we are. All we have to do is look at our lives.

It appears that Jesus is calling us to choose whether we will hear and obey (which will protect us from the storms), or whether we hear and ignore. I have been there, brothers. I have been awash in the storm of the earthly death of my two-and-a-half-year-old. I will tell you first-hand that if my wife and I did not know the words of Jesus Christ and had not put them into practice, we would not have survived. Decide today to be a wise man before the storms come.

FOR REFLECTION

What is your attitude toward reading the Bible? Is it something you love? Or something you are indifferent about? Make it a point today to take your Bible study to the next level, whatever that looks like for you. Don't wait until it's too late.

DAY 27

WHAT IS YOUR NAME?

"[27] And he said to him, 'What is your name?' And he said, 'Jacob.' [28] Then he said, 'Your name shall no longer be called Jacob, but Israel, for you have striven with God and with men, and have prevailed.'" - GENESIS 32:27-28

Open your Bible to Genesis 32. There is so much going on here that ties to our ongoing study on being transformed. Jacob has finally freed himself from his father-in-law Laban. He is returning to Canaan. He had been gone since Rebecca snuck him out when his brother Esau sought to kill him after Jacob cheated Esau out of his father's blessing.

Do you remember the story? Even though they were twins, Esau was born first and Jacob second. Even though Jacob was born second, God promised Rebecca that Esau would serve Jacob because God had chosen Jacob not Esau to be the child through which His ongoing covenant with Abraham would be honored. God made His decision that Jacob would receive the blessing, but Rebecca and Jacob got tired of waiting on God and devised their plan to cheat Esau out of the blessing. Esau was angry and vowed to kill Jacob, so Rebecca sent him to Haran to live with Laban.

It's a complex story, made even more so by Jacob's actions. But Jacob would soon receive a dose of his own medicine. Laban would deceive the deceiver, keeping Jacob in his employ for 20 years after Laban double-crossed him in regard to marrying his daughters, Leah and Rachel. So we pick up the story in chapter 32. God has freed Jacob from Laban, and Jacob is headed back to the land God promised to his family. One problem: the last time he saw Esau, he wanted to kill Jacob.

Jacob is afraid that Esau still wants to kill him, but Jacob wants to reconcile. So, he devises a plan to determine if Esau is still angry. Jacob is certain that his struggle is with Esau, but in verses 22-31, Jacob has an encounter with God that would transform him.

Jacob is alone, waiting on his encounter with his brother Esau, only to discover that his conflict is actually with God. Moses tells us in Genesis 32:24 that Jacob was alone and wrestled with a man until the day's breaking. When the man could not prevail against Jacob, he touched the hip socket and put it out of joint. The fact that all the "man" had to do was touch Jacob's hip to remove it from the joint tells us quickly that Jacob is wrestling with God in the form of a man. Jacob begs to be blessed, and God says to Jacob, "What is your name?" He replied, "Jacob." Now Jacob's name means "he takes by the heel," which is another way of saying "he cheats" or "he deceives." Which up to this point, has seemed a fitting name for Jacob. But God is in the transformation business, and that's exactly what happened.

God performed a name-change on Jacob, which we know from Scripture means much more than just a change on someone's ID. It means a completely new purpose. God told Jacob his name would be Israel. Did you catch all that is going on here? God called Jacob to repent of his sin of deceiving his father and brother. Jacob was there in the first place, gripped with fear because he had worked his own plan. Look what it caused. Jacob has been gone from the land God promised Jacob's grandfather (Abraham), father (Isaac), and now Jacob himself for 20 years because of his deception. God was changing the narrative by confronting Jacob's past.

By the way, don't miss the significance of touching the hip. Jewish males believed this area of the body housed their strength and vitality. God simply touched it to knock it out of joint. Who had the upper hand? God, of course, but He allowed Jacob to wrestle this out. What does Jacob beg for? God's blessing. Why? Because he knew he worked his plan, and it didn't work out. He begged God to give him a second chance to receive the blessing the right way.

The grace of god was so prominent when He asked Jacob his name! Do we think God didn't know his name? He is calling Jacob to repentance so He can have a new name. His name was "the cheater." God said, "not anymore; you get a new name because you have been transformed through your struggle to beg me for forgiveness."

Notice God chooses not to heal the hip. Jacob was left with a limp. Why? Couldn't God heal the limp? Yes, but He left it to remind Jacob of his struggle and how God redeemed him. It kept him humble.

So what is your name? Watcher of porn? Liar? Adulterer? Fornicator? Thief? Coward? Well, if you are willing to repent and acknowledge your sin, God will forgive you and give you a new name. God transforms. He heals. He redeems. But it starts with your repentance. What are you waiting on?

FOR REFLECTION

During the struggle, don't miss that God tells Jacob to let Him go before the break of day. Why? To see God's face would have meant death for Jacob. Work whatever you need to out with God before it's too late. God will forgive all who sincerely repent, but a day is coming when the season of God's grace will be over, and the season of judgment will be upon creation. We do not want to face God without the redemption found in Jesus. Don't wait. Repent and be ready to accept a new purpose from the Lord.

DAY 28
ABIDE IN ME

"Abide in me, and I in you. As the branch cannot bear fruit by itself, unless it abides in the vine, neither can you, unless you abide in me." -JOHN 15:4

As a man, I know we want to be handed the game plan. My wife gets frustrated with me when I make my (according to her) predictable statement about getting our plan for whatever we are about to do. For example, when Christmas is approaching, I will say something like "OK, what's our plan for Christmas eve this year" or "What's the plan for this coming weekend," etc. So when men read in John 15 that Jesus is teaching His disciples about the call to grow up spiritually, they want to be given a plan. Well, Jesus does just that.

In John 15:4, Jesus' strategy for transformation is for us to take on a "one-step plan" called abiding in Him. We have already touched on this, but let's review what the word abide means. The definition calls for us to act in accordance with or to make a decision to remain. It is not a casual relationship. In John 15, Jesus uses the analogy of Himself as the True Vine. In Psalm 80, the psalmist refers to God taking His people out of Egypt as though they were a tender vine. God then planted them in the promised land to take root. Jesus is telling the disciples and any who would listen that He is the True Vine and that He will deliver us from the bondage of sin. This is a powerful statement from Jesus one that would have sent ripples through His audience.

Jesus then instructed His disciples to abide in Him as He abides in us because we need His power to produce the fruit of the Spirit in our lives. It's a one-step program. We must intentionally act in accordance with Jesus to access His power that transforms us by producing fruit that we cannot produce.

Every man reading this devotional must understand that a new set of rules or some newfound self-control cannot change us. We cannot produce this fruit in our life. Jesus says plainly that we cannot bear this fruit on our own strength. So stop being frustrated by a process that isn't going to work. Abide in Christ. Period.

We tend to think we need to get our act together to abide in Christ, who will accept us because we finally got it together. Jesus says this plan will not work. We must simply repent of our sins, acknowledge we can do nothing to save ourselves, and immerse ourselves in Christ through prayer, involvement in His church (not just attending), worshipping Him, being about His business, and being students of His Word. His power changes us.

Imagine saying that your car needs fuel, so you park next to a gasoline pump, hoping the car will be filled. That wouldn't make any sense. You have to take action. You must take the hose from the pump, place it into the car, and pull the handle. We don't have the fuel; we are accessing the fuel. The same is true in our faith. We fuel ourselves by abiding in Jesus.

Now take time to look at verse 5. Jesus goes on to ensure we understand the importance of abiding in Him. He says that he that abides in Him produces much fruit (transformation), for apart from Him, we can do nothing. Do you get that, brother? Apart from abiding in Jesus, we can't pull this off. But He is so powerful that if we abide in Him, He will produce not some but much fruit.

FOR REFLECTION

Look at verse 6. Jesus talks about those trying to stand before the father as branches not connected to the vine. Since these people did not connect themselves to the True Vine, they are withered and good for only one thing, and it's not good. Do not attempt to be the branch that will try to stand before a perfect and holy God without being connected to the True Vine. Make sure you are connected to the vine and live out of this identity.

DAY 29
THE RIGHT THINGS

"[7] If you abide in me, and my words abide in you, ask whatever you wish, and it will be done for you. [8] By this my Father is glorified, that you bear much fruit and so prove to be my disciples." -JOHN 15:7-8

We continue today with the concept of abiding in Jesus in order to be transformed. Jesus makes an interesting statement here that sadly has often been abused and used by heretics to preach a false Gospel. Let's be sure we get this correct by looking at what Jesus is not saying.

Jesus is not saying that if we are redeemed, we can ask Him for anything, and if we do it right and have enough faith, He will give it to us. Jesus is talking about how His power completely transforms us into something less like us and more like Him. Jesus has already told us that He came to this earth to do His father's will; as His disciples, we should follow His example.

Have you noticed that we begin to act like the people we spend the most time around? This is why as parents, we are always concerned about the inner circle of friends where our children spend most of their time. Why? Because they usually become like them and even develop their taste and choices of their friends. One of the humorous things I notice about young people who say they want to be so unique may reject the styles of their parents only to adopt the styles of their friends. They aren't unique; they just change the group they want to identify with. Jesus states that if we truly abide in Him, we will adopt His desires, not ours.

This is an important truth that we must realize. When Jesus redeems us, He isn't trying to give us our desires; He is changing our desires to be what He desires. So Jesus is stating here quite plainly that abiding in Him will so change our desires that we begin to ask Him for the right things that are in the will of God, which He will give us. Jesus isn't going to give us our desires until our desires are rightly in line with the will of God. But when that happens, He will give them to us. He will transform us so that we stop asking for the wrong things!

Then Jesus reminds us that this transformation causes us to produce much fruit, proving that we are His disciples. Jesus says that bearing much fruit is proof of the validity of our claim to be His disciple. We must ask ourselves what our lives say about our fruitfulness.

FOR REFLECTION

If someone looked into our lives, would they see the proof of our discipleship? Based on the fruit that flows from our lives, is the validity of our claim to be a disciple of Jesus confirmed? If not, then maybe we are not abiding in Him, which is why our desires still conflict with Him. Maybe it's time to stop asking Jesus for the wrong things and start abiding in Him until we become so much like Him we ask for only the things that please God.

DAY 30
MAKING DISCIPLES

"[18] And Jesus came and said to them, 'All authority in heaven and on earth has been given to me. [19] Go therefore and make disciples of all nations, baptizing them in the name of the Father and of the Son and of the Holy Spirit, [20] teaching them to observe all that I have commanded you. And behold, I am with you always, to the end of the age.'" -MATTHEW 28:18-20

As we have walked through the last 29 days together, Scripture clearly states that obedience and legalism are not the same. Obedience certainly doesn't earn us salvation, but Jesus repeatedly says that it is proof of salvation. Jesus says in John 14 that those who love Him obey Him and those who do not love Him do not obey Him. Jesus says in Matthew 7 that only those who do the will of the Father are His true disciples, and the rest just claim to be. Jesus says in John 15 that if we abide in Him, He will produce much fruit in us, proving that we are His disciples. True disciples of Jesus say what He says to say and do what He says to do. Paul tells us in 2 Corinthians 13:5-6 that we should examine ourselves to see if we are really of the faith, look at our lives, and assess whether or not we see the proof of Jesus in our lives.

In today's passage, Jesus is teaching His disciples after the resurrection and making sure they understand what to continue to do until their earthly death or His return. So these instructions are some of the last words taught by Jesus on earth. This seems to be very important.

Read the Scripture again. Jesus says He expects all who claim to be His disciples to now make disciples, baptizing them in the name of the Father, Son, and Holy Spirit and teaching them all He has commanded us. So now the question is, "Are you doing this"?

Jesus again has said that His true disciples do what He commands. Is there anyone who would say that you and I made them a disciple of Jesus? And that we had or are teaching them to obey His commands? First, we must know what Jesus commanded because that appears crucial to making a disciple. So, let's pause and realize that even if we want to make disciples, we won't be successful if we don't know what to teach them. I can't teach someone something that I don't know.

Maybe today is the day we take a hard look at our lives and ask ourselves how obedient we have been to this command. Maybe it's time we drop the excuses. Jesus did not say that we are to make disciples and teach them all He commanded unless it's not our personality. He said He would not command us to do anything He did not have the power to accomplish through our simple obedience.

We don't have to have a seminary degree to tell someone how faith in Christ has radically changed our lives. Do we see the power of Jesus in the new creation we have become? Are we growing from spiritual infancy to spiritual maturity due to our pursuit of Jesus, who totally fulfills our lives like nothing else seems to do? Do we have that desire, or do we neglect to make disciples of Jesus because we're worshipping sports teams, workouts, nutrition, books, TV shows, movies, music, money, or our children's accomplishments?

We do know how to make disciples; we just too often make disciples of the wrong things. Maybe it's time to repent of this attitude.

FOR REFLECTION

What if today you finally came out from under your own authority and completely submitted to God? Tell Him that you know that He loves you; He made that clear on the cross. But now, ask Him to teach you to love Him because you will finally obey Him when you love Him.

DAY 31
FINISHING THE COURSE

"But I do not account my life of any value nor as precious to myself, if only I may finish my course and the ministry that I received from the Lord Jesus, to testify to the gospel of the grace of God." -ACTS 20:24

You have reached day 31. With this in mind, we will close this devotional with Paul's final words to the Ephesian elders. Paul acknowledges that they will likely never see his face again, but he relishes the fact that he has lived his life with integrity; he has told them the truth, and if they reject it, then their blood will not be on his hands, because he had told them the whole counsel of God (Acts 20:26). But first Paul tells them about his example.

Paul tells the Ephesians that he does not consider his life of any value if he does not finish the ministry that Christ called him to fulfill. He must testify to the Gospel and the grace of God. He doesn't consider anything else to be more important. This attitude comes from the fact that Paul has been transformed from his former self. Think about that for a moment; Paul once persecuted the very Church that he now advanced. He had an encounter with Jesus, and that encounter so transformed him that he not only loves the followers of Jesus, he has become one of His most dedicated followers.

Has this happened to you? I remember the person I was before I finally repented of my sin, left faith in myself, placed my faith in Jesus, and died to myself. Once I sincerely desired to be redeemed and transformed, Jesus began to turn me into a man that is nothing like the man who finally died. I went from bar hopping to standing in a circle with old men who would spend their Monday nights going door-to-door telling people about Jesus. I could not believe what was happening to me. I wanted to be with them, and due to the power of the Holy Spirit, I went from having no desire to be in a church to craving to be in worship and hungry for the Word. If you can't say the same thing, then something is wrong.

Do you believe your life is of no value unless you finish the work Christ has called you to? This is so very important. Do you desire to be about the business of advancing the Kingdom of God? Every single person must answer the call that Christ places on their life. Every one of us has been called to something. There is no such thing as a call from God to do nothing. Are we attending church, or are we serving the church? Has our faith in Christ cost us anything? If our bodies were to be buried today, what would our family and friends say about our impact on the Kingdom of God? We cannot finish a course that we have never decided to begin.

Are you ready to begin? Are you ready to answer God's call on your life? For the last 31 days, we have looked at our lives to see if we see evidence that we have truly been transformed by the power that only Jesus provides. So as we have examined ourselves, we must now take action to change any aspect of our spiritual life that needs to be addressed.

FOR REFLECTION

Let me offer one last challenge. If we do not see the evidence of the power of Christ in our lives, then we must not be too prideful or afraid to consider that the issue might simply be that we are just lost. If we claim that we have been redeemed, then we must be willing to look at the evidence that is our life and honestly assess whether or not the claim of redemption can be validated. If you don't pass the test, maybe today for the first time or the first time you are truly sincere, you need to repent of your sin and sincerely place your faith completely in Christ. If this describes you, don't wait. Leave our authority and submit to the authority of Christ alone. Confess your faith in Jesus (Romans 10:9-10). And decide to die to yourself and be transformed by Christ (Luke 9:23). It is the most important decision you will ever make.

Rick Burgess has been the cohost of the "Rick and Bubba Show" since 1994, a nationally syndicated radio show which airs to 1.2 million people weekly. Rick has coauthored multiple New York Times bestselling books, the "How To Be A Man" series of 40-day devotionals, and numerous articles. As a commentator and guest, Rick has appeared on various radio and television shows, including "Fox and Friends" and the "Sean Hannity Show".

Rick is a frequent speaker at church services and youth and marriage conferences, but his true passion is men's ministry. As Founder of The Man Church, Rick calls on the modern church to put into practice what they say every Father's Day, that a man's family will follow him if he leads them.

He has been married to the former Sherri Bodine since 1996. Rick's Spirit-filled message at his youngest son's memorial service was the most-watched YouTube video in the world the week it was posted.

Many men struggle with their daily Bible reading time.

These books can change that.

One of the most common spiritual challenges men face is building a consistent daily Bible reading habit. Most men have the desire, but they don't know where to start.

Iron Hill Press' line of daily devotionals are Bible-centered, Gospel-driven resources that will challenge men to become who God intends them to be.

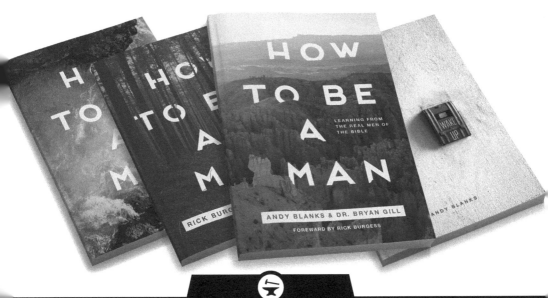

IRON HILL

press

Iron Hill Press is a collective of people who love Jesus, love Gospel truth, and love sharing those things with others through the medium of publishing and gospel-centered event experiences. Learn more about us at ironhillpress.com.

ironhillpress.com   888.969.6360